Sch

D0419528

COPING WITH
BULLYING

Charlotte Guillain

www.raintreepublishers.co.uk
Visit our website to find out
more information about
Raintree books.

To order:
☎ Phone 0845 6044371
🗎 Fax +44 (0) 1865 312263
✉ Email myorders@raintreepublishers.co.uk

Customers from outside the UK please telephone +44 1865 312262

©Raintree is an imprint of Capstone Global Library
Limited, a company incorporated in England and
Wales having its registered office at 7 Pilgrim Street,
London, EC4V 6LB – Registered company number:
6695582

Text © Capstone Global Library Limited 2011
First published in hardback in 2011
The moral rights of the proprietor have been
asserted. All rights reserved.

No part of this publication may be reproduced in
any form or by any means (including photocopying
or storing it in any medium by electronic means
and whether or not transiently or incidentally to
some other use of this publication) without the
written permission of the copyright owner, except
in accordance with the provisions of the Copyright,
Designs and Patents Act 1988 or under the terms of
a licence issued by the Copyright Licensing Agency,
Saffron House, 6–10 Kirby Street, London EC1N
8TS (www.cla.co.uk). Applications for the copyright
owner's written permission should be addressed to
the publisher.

Edited by Louise Galpine and Laura Knowles
Designed by Richard Parker
Original illustrations © Capstone Global Library
    Ltd 2011
Picture research by Liz Alexander
Originated by Capstone Global Library Ltd
Printed and bound in China by South China
    Printing Company Ltd

ISBN 978 1 406 21984 5 (hardback)
15 14 13 12 11
10 9 8 7 6 5 4 3 2 1

British Library Cataloguing in Publication Data
Guillain, Charlotte.
Coping with bullying. -- (Real life issues)
155.9'2-dc22
A full catalogue record for this book is available
from the British Library.

Northamptonshire Libraries & Information Service	
60 000 117 045	
Peters	17-Mar-2011
302.5	£13.49

Acknowledgements
We would like to thank the following for
permission to reproduce photographs: Alamy
pp. **8** (© Angela Hampton Picture Library), **11**
(© Design Pics Inc.), **15** (© Kuttig – People),
16 (© Radius Images), **21** (© Geof Kirby), **23**
(© mark phillips), **30** (© Catchlight Visual Services),
33 (© imagebroker), **34** (© Angela Hampton Picture
Library), **38** (© Bob Pardue - Teen Lifestyle); Corbis
pp. **7** (© Jim Craigmyle), **17** (© Image Source),
19 (© Nick White/cultura), **28** (© Lou Cypher),
43 (© LWA/Dann Tardif/Blend Images); Getty
Images p. **18** (Justin Pumfrey/Taxi); Photolibrary
pp. **5** (Peter Brooker), **6** (Polka Dot Images), **10**
(PureStock), **12** (Leah Warkentin/Design Pics Inc),
13 (Ray Tang), **25** (Banana Stock), **27** (Eyecandy
Images), **37** (Sonny T Senser/age fotostock), **39**
(Richard Hutchings/Digital Light Source), **41**
(Laurence Mouton/Photoalto); Shutterstock p. **35**
(© Galina Barskaya).

"Distressed texture" design detail reproduced with
permission of iStockphoto/© Diana Walters.

Cover photograph of two teenage boys stealing items
from schoolgirl's bag reproduced with permission of
Photolibrary/Chris Whitehead/White.

Graph on page 9 produced from data collected by
the National Centre for Social Research and the
Department for Education.

We would like to thank Anne Pezalla for her
invaluable help in the preparation of this book.

Every effort has been made to contact copyright
holders of material reproduced in this book. Any
omissions will be rectified in subsequent printings if
notice is given to the publishers.

In order to protect the privacy of individuals, some
names in this book have been changed.

Disclaimer
All the Internet addresses (URLs) given in this book
were valid at the time of going to press. However,
due to the dynamic nature of the Internet, some
addresses may have changed, or sites may have
changed or ceased to exist since publication. While
the author and publisher regret any inconvenience
this may cause readers, no responsibility for any
such changes can be accepted by either the author or
the publisher.

CONTENTS

Stay safe on the internet!
When you are on the internet, never give personal details such as your real name, phone number, or address to anyone you have only had contact with online. If you are contacted by anyone who makes you feel uncomfortable or upset, don't reply to them, tell an adult, and block that person from contacting you again.

Any words appearing in the text in bold, **like this**, are explained in the glossary.

Have you ever seen bullying or been bullied yourself? What exactly is bullying? If people are left out or called names, this is bullying. **Cyber** bullies use the internet or mobile phones to say nasty things about someone. Some bullies post private or upsetting photos and videos of people on websites. Other bullies **physically** hurt people, sometimes breaking the law. All of these actions are harmful and can be more damaging to the **victims** than the bullies ever imagine.

How this book can help

As you read this book you might realize that you have been bullied or even been a bully yourself. In either case you'll want to make a change. You might recognize types of bullying that you have seen at your school and you might not have known what to do. This book will support anyone who is being bullied and provide information about organizations that can help. It will give people who see bullying useful ideas on how to act and not just stand by. It should make people consider whether they have been bullies themselves, and think about the impact their actions have on others.

CASE STUDY

Even celebrities can be victims of bullying. The singer Taylor Swift was miserable at secondary school because she was picked on. *Twilight* actor Taylor Lautner was also teased at school, and N Dubz singer Tulisa suffered cyber bullying on her MySpace page.

Singer Taylor Swift was a victim of bullying when she was younger.

Verbal bullying

Everyone likes to make their friends laugh and often people make jokes about the way others look or behave. We all make these sorts of jokes sometimes. If the person you are teasing doesn't mind, then it's okay. But have you ever been teased about the same thing again and again? The joke stops being funny and it can be upsetting. This kind of teasing can make people feel shy and **self-conscious** and it can stop other children seeing what they are really like.

It is only okay to tease and make jokes about people if you are being friendly and you are sure they are happy with it. If you can see someone is getting annoyed, you should always stop and think about their feelings. Think how you would feel if you were being picked on in this way.

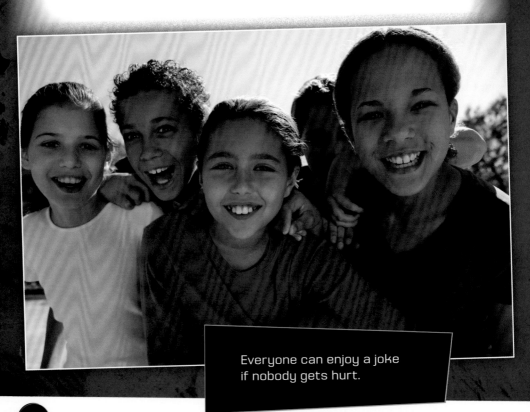

Everyone can enjoy a joke if nobody gets hurt.

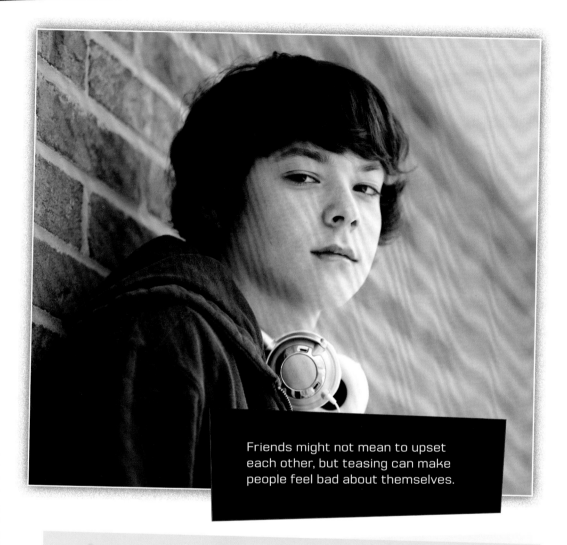

Friends might not mean to upset each other, but teasing can make people feel bad about themselves.

CASE STUDY

Kelli was teased at school because she has a **birthmark** on her face. She told her teachers about the teasing but nothing seemed to change. So she talked to her parents and they went to the school to speak to the head teacher. He took it very seriously and talked to the bullies and their parents. If they had continued picking on Kelli they would have been **suspended** from school. Kelli felt supported and the bullying stopped for good.

"Sticks and stones"

It is very easy for teasing and picking on people to go further and become **verbal** bullying. This type of bullying can include calling someone names or even ignoring them and leaving them out. You might not think this is serious, but it can be very hurtful. When a group of classmates doesn't include someone, it can make that person feel very lonely. Many young people start to think there is something wrong with them. This can make it difficult for them to make new friends. Even if you don't get along with someone, it is important to be friendly and remember they have feelings.

Have you ever been left out of a group? How did it make you feel?

BEHIND THE HEADLINES

The charity ChildLine and the government did some research into bullying and discovered that over 54 per cent of schoolchildren thought bullying was "a big problem" or "quite a big problem" in their school. However, as pupils get older the amount of bullying seems to go down. Recent reports have also shown that young people who talk to their parents about bullying are more likely to stop suffering because the problem can be sorted out. So the message is, if you are being bullied, speak out and tell an adult you trust. You are not alone.

This bar chart shows the percentage of UK pupils aged 14 who reported being bullied at school in 2009.

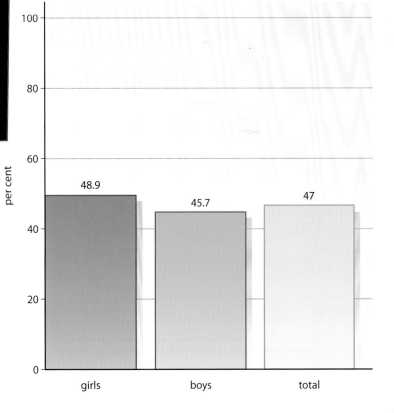

Rumours and threats

Verbal bullying can also include spreading nasty **rumours** about someone. If you hear unkind gossip about a classmate, stop the rumour and do not pass it on. If you think rumours are being spread about you, tell a teacher straight away.

Another type of verbal bullying is **threatening** and **intimidating** people. Often when bullies threaten a **victim**, these threats can lead to **physical** bullying, where someone is actually hurt.

It is best to stop bullying early on. If you see someone spreading rumours or threatening others, don't ignore it. Tell a trusted adult. If you are being bullied in this way, do the same. Your school will have a system for dealing with bullies and your teachers need to know what is going on.

It is never nice to feel people are talking about you behind your back. If someone tells you a rumour, choose not to pass it on.

Online!

If you are being bullied you can find organizations online that will help and support you.

- Visit the Childline website (see page 46) and talk to someone about what is worrying you. They will give you help and advice. You can also look on their **message boards** to link up with other kids who are being bullied, so you won't feel so alone.

- Beatbullying's website (see page 46) has plenty of advice. They have ideas on how to lead anti-bullying campaigns and can even help you if you think you might be a bully.

It is never okay to threaten other people.

Physical bullying

Sometimes bullying can move from name-calling and **verbal** threats to **physical** bullying. Physical bullying could be something as simple as pushing other children about. Bullies sometimes take or damage other people's belongings. You might enjoy joking around with your friends but it is important to know when to stop. If your classmates mess around with your things and upset you, or you are tired of being pushed around, make sure you tell them how you feel. They might think they are just having fun and will stop if they know you have had enough. If they carry on then you should talk to a teacher.

Always tell an adult straight away if you are bullied physically.

Tom Daley was picked on at school after he became famous at the Beijing Olympics.

BEHIND THE HEADLINES

Tom Daley was the youngest diving finalist at the 2008 Olympics and became a world diving champion at the age of 15. Unfortunately, Tom was bullied at school. It reached the point where Tom couldn't go outside at break time because one bully had threatened to break his legs. He had four good friends who stuck with him through the bullying, but in the end Tom moved to another school. He hasn't forgotten his experience and supports ChildLine, an organization that helps other children who are suffering from bullying and other problems.

Peter Bradley, from the charity Kidscape, says: "Tom was brave in telling others he was having trouble. We hope that all young people will realize that the first step to breaking the chain of bullying is asking for help, and refusing to let the bullies win."

Getting violent

Physical bullying can be **violent**. Sometimes bullies kick, hit, or hurt people in other ways. This bullying can become very serious when **victims** are injured, and it can make some young people afraid to go to school or go outside in their free time.

It is very important that you tell a teacher or other adult if a bully attacks you or you see someone hurting another person. The quicker this behaviour is stopped, the less likely it is to happen again. When bullies are reported quickly, other people may think twice before hurting others.

CASE STUDY

Danni was bullied at primary school when she fell out with a friend. Things got really nasty when someone banged a heavy door into her head. The bullying carried on when Danni started secondary school, when she was hit round the face and **threatened** with a broken bottle. Danni was even scared when she was out of school because the bullying carried on in the holidays and stopped her from going out.

Finally Danni told her teachers. They took action to make sure the bullies faced **consequences** for their behaviour. Danni was offered **counselling**, where she learned how to deal with the bullying, and she moved to a different class. Now things are much better and at last she is enjoying school.

Violence is not an acceptable way of showing your feelings.

Gangs

Violent physical bullying can become very serious when gangs are involved. In many cities, kids who are part of a gang outside school bring their problems to class. Many people are concerned about the number of students taking knives to school with them. These weapons can lead to dangerous attacks both in school and on the way to and from school. In other places, gang violence is not so extreme but can still make some children too scared to go to school.

Many young people feel pressure to join a gang to fit in and to feel protected. In fact, gang members are more likely to be involved in violence and bullying. This means it is safer to avoid gangs.

Young people who get involved in gangs could find themselves or their friends getting seriously injured.

Joining a gang won't keep you safe from bullying.

BEHIND THE HEADLINES

The government is helping schools to spot pupils who are thinking about joining gangs. Their plan is to stop young people before they get too involved in gang violence. If schools think that a pupil is likely to join a gang there are ways that the teachers, police, and youth workers can help and support him or her to stop this happening. The number of pupils carrying knives in school has increased in recent years. When knives are used in fights it can lead to people being killed. This is a growing problem in some cities in the United Kingdom. **Campaigns** such as an anti-knife crime week help to make young people think about the dangers of joining gangs and carrying knives.

Mobile phone bullying

In the past, some children were unlucky enough to suffer bullying at school, but at least they were safe when they returned home. Now, modern technology means that it is possible for bullies to **intimidate** and **abuse** their **victims** at any time. One of the ways bullies do this is by using mobile phones.

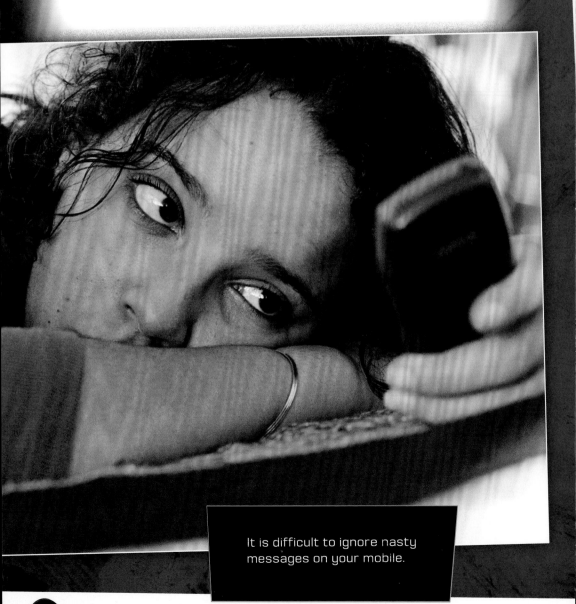

It is difficult to ignore nasty messages on your mobile.

Some bullies send nasty text messages that insult or **threaten** people, often without showing the name of the sender. Other bullies call their victims and shout abuse when the phone is answered, or don't say anything at all. This type of behaviour may seem like a funny joke, but the calls can make the child being bullied feel that he or she is never safe. These calls can also be against the law. Always tell your parents or teachers if you or a friend is bullied in this way. It is best to stop the problem early on.

Abusive calls and text messages can make people's lives miserable. It is best to tell a trusted adult.

CASE STUDY

Lisa was careful about giving her mobile phone number to people. But when she fell out with a friend, she received mean text messages insulting how she looked and spoke. Lisa's first reaction was to text back and tell the bully to stop, but this made things worse. After weeks of texts she was very upset and told her parents. They helped her stop the bullying. Lisa's advice is to tell an adult as soon as you get bullying messages and they will help you to solve the problem. Never text back because this will only encourage the bullies.

Photos and video

Mobile phone bullying goes further when people take photos or make videos. Many young people have embarrassing pictures or videos of them sent to their schoolmates by bullies. These images can be very personal and upsetting. It is horrible for anyone to know that they are being laughed at, so never be tempted to take these pictures, even if it seems to be just a joke. If you receive a nasty image of someone, let an adult know and delete it. Never send it on or show other people.

You should also be very careful of the pictures you share of yourself. You might take pictures for a friend, boyfriend, or girlfriend that you wouldn't want other people to see, but these photos could get into the wrong hands. Stay safe and only share pictures of yourself that you would be happy for your parents and teachers to see.

BEHIND THE HEADLINES

Sending some photos by mobile phone can be a serious crime. In January 2010 a 14-year-old boy in Washington, USA was arrested. He had sent a naked photograph of his 13-year-old girlfriend to classmates using his mobile phone. In the end, teenagers at three different schools saw the photos. Sending images such as this is a crime and anyone doing it can be punished, perhaps even with prison. Over 30 per cent of teenagers admit they swap these sorts of photos, so many young people are risking getting into trouble.

Think how you would feel if people were laughing at pictures of you.

Bullying on the internet

As well as mobile phones, bullies can also use the internet to hurt people. This type of bullying is often called "**cyber** bullying", and includes sending nasty emails or messages on **social networking sites** or in **chat rooms**. Other bullies pretend to be their **victims** online, and send embarrassing or rude messages to their friends and other people to cause trouble. The internet is another place where unkind photos and videos can be shared. This can be hurtful and is sometimes against the law.

The internet is a way for bullies to reach their victims when they are at home as well as at school. Young people who are targeted online by bullies can feel very lonely and upset. It can seem that there is no escape from the bullies. Some victims of internet bullying stop going to school. Missing lessons can cause them long-lasting damage. Occasionally, teenagers have felt so hopeless after internet bullying that they have been desperate enough to kill themselves.

BEHIND THE HEADLINES

Megan Meier was 13 years old when she killed herself. She had been in touch with a boy called Josh on the social networking site MySpace. Josh had been friendly at first, but then he turned against her. He posted abusive messages about Megan and made her feel desperately unhappy. After Megan's death it was discovered that "Josh" didn't actually exist but had been created by a neighbourhood family. Terrible stories like this one show how serious the effects of internet bullying can be.

Cyber bullying can ruin
people's lives.

Hate pages

Some young people have become the victim of hate pages on the internet. These are web pages where **rumours** and nasty comments about someone are posted along with photographs. When victims see these hate pages they can think that everyone they know hates them. Many victims feel desperate and **insecure**. Perhaps bullies who make hate pages think they are funny, but the effects can be very serious. If you know that people are creating a hate page about someone, you should tell a teacher or other trusted adult.

Leaving a trail

People who use the internet to bully and upset other people might think they are safe because nobody can see them. In fact, everything posted online can be traced and bullies can be found. All the evidence of this type of bullying is available for anyone to see. Even if you are not bullying others on the internet, you should still be careful about everything you post online because you never know who will end up seeing your pictures or reading your messages.

Online!

The internet can be used to bully people, but it can also be on your side. If you are bullied through a social networking site, a chat room, or email, there will be people who run these services to whom you can report the bullying. Even if the bullies try to be clever and hide their identity, they can still be traced. Everything they post on the internet can be linked to them, even if it has been deleted.

Talk about it

Anyone who is being cyber bullied should tell someone what is happening. Always speak to a trusted adult, such as a parent or teacher, if you receive or see anything online that upsets you. If you try to ignore the problem or send messages back to the bully, you might start to feel very isolated and scared.

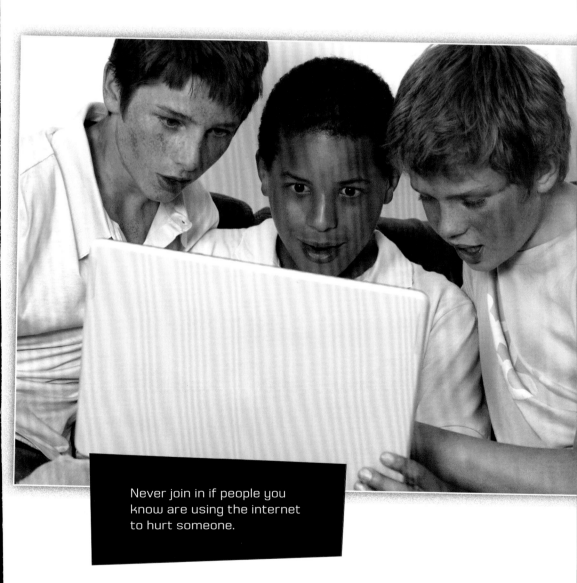

Never join in if people you know are using the internet to hurt someone.

Zip it, block it, flag it

When you are using the internet remember to "zip it, block it, flag it". Zip it by never replying to the bullies and staying calm. The next step is to block the people who are bullying you so they can no longer reach your email address or social networking pages. The most important step is to flag up the problem with a parent or teacher who can support you in getting the bullies out of your life. It is also best only to use the internet when a parent or another adult you trust is with you.

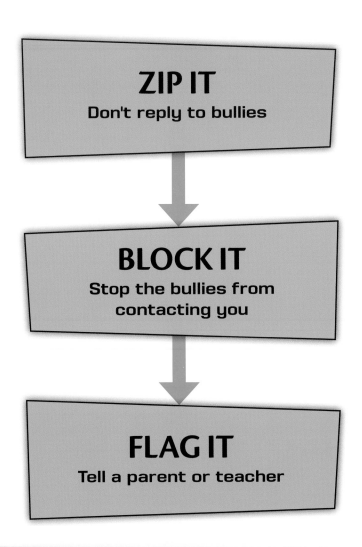

ZIP IT
Don't reply to bullies

BLOCK IT
Stop the bullies from contacting you

FLAG IT
Tell a parent or teacher

Online!

It is very important to make sure you stay safe when you use the internet:

- If someone you have never met face-to-face contacts you, never tell them your real name, age, school, or home address.
- Never agree to meet someone you have only met online unless your parents know who they are and go to the meeting with you.
- Choose your screen name carefully so it doesn't have anything to do with your real name.
- If someone is rude to you online then do not reply.

You can take control back from the bullies.

Why do people bully?

There is no single reason why bullies pick on others. Some bullies might think they are having fun and don't realize they are hurting other people. They might want to make their classmates laugh at the expense of someone else. Other bullies might think the bullying will make them popular or cool. Some bullies might have been picked on themselves in the past, so they could be angry or wanting **revenge** or attention.

There is no excuse for picking on someone. How would it make you feel?

WHAT DO YOU THINK?

If you see a bully picking on someone, what should you do?

Ignore the bullying?	Tell a trusted adult?
If you tell a teacher then the bully might start picking on you, but...	... if nobody gets help the bullying could get worse.
You might not be popular if you stand up to a bully, but...	... if the bully thinks they are safe they might start picking on other people, perhaps you.
If you keep your head down the bully might not notice you, but ...	... no bullying is acceptable and if everyone stands together against it then it will stop.

Whatever the reason, it is never right to bully other people. Many people who bully others don't realize this is what they are doing. It is important to stop any teasing that gets out of hand before things get worse. The only way to stop bullying is for everyone who sees it to speak up and say that it is not okay. Be brave, get help, and don't accept it.

Behind the bullying

Other bullies might have more serious problems of their own. Perhaps they are experiencing violence or other **abuse** at home. They might be feeling upset about something and hurting other people is their way of taking control. Some bullies might be jealous of their classmates and take their frustration out on them by bullying.

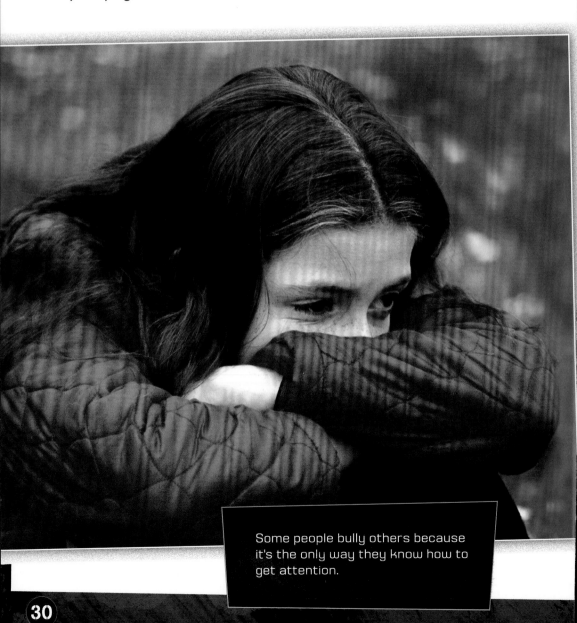

Some people bully others because it's the only way they know how to get attention.

Bullies need help

None of these reasons for bullying is acceptable, but it is important to understand that most bullies have problems too. Telling a teacher or another adult about any bullying you see is important because not only will the **victim** be helped, but perhaps the bully will get help too.

CASE STUDY

What do you do when you feel angry or upset about something? Here are some ways other young people deal with their anger without taking it out on others:

- Becky takes a few deep breaths when she feels angry and thinks of good thoughts. She tries to remember that it ruins your day if you waste it being angry.

- When Connor is angry he takes his dog down to the beach and relaxes.

- Carla tries to let out her anger in a way that won't hurt any one or break anything. Sometimes she punches a pillow, kicks a fence, or stamps around the house. When she's done that she can talk about it.

- When Rashid gets too worked up, he goes to his room and listens to music until he calms down.

Could you be a bully?

You probably think you are not a bully. But have you ever gossiped about a classmate or spread **rumours**? Have you ever sent emails that make fun of someone or called anyone names? Maybe you have played jokes on someone who looks or behaves a bit differently? You might not think this behaviour is serious, but how might the person you are picking on feel? Would you like to feel like that? Always question whether your behaviour is going to make someone unhappy. If you don't think about this, you could become a bully.

Maybe you know you are a bully. Remember that **physically** attacking someone else is a **criminal offence** and could get you into trouble. Making abusive phone calls and sharing certain photos or videos could also be against the law. Just because you have bullied before does not mean you have to carry on behaving in that way. It's never too late to change and give yourself a better future.

CASE STUDY

Liam started getting into trouble when he was at primary school. Other kids wound him up and he would react by lashing out at them. His sister was being bullied and this made Liam angry and **aggressive**. When he was 14, his mum was shown a video of Liam violently kicking another child at school. Liam was **excluded** from school but he still insisted that he was not a bully. When Liam calmed down he finally admitted he was a bully and agreed to work with his mum to deal with the problem.

Be honest with yourself. If you have bullied other people in the past, now is the time to stop.

Coping with bullying

Never ignore bullying. Even if you are not being bullied yourself, it is still important to make sure you and your friends don't **tolerate** any bullying you see. If bullies know that most people don't like what they are doing, they are more likely to stop. When bullies know they will be reported and face **consequences**, bullying doesn't seem like such a fun or easy thing to do.

Your school should have a system to deal with bullying. If you don't think the system is working, you and your classmates can talk to your teachers and the school council about tackling the bullying in your school. If you all work together then nobody should be scared of bullies.

Everyone at your school can work together to stop bullying.

Make time to
listen to friends
who feel bullied.

WHAT DO YOU THINK?

Do you think the best way to stop bullying is to help bullies deal with
their own problems? Or do you think they just need to be punished?

Punish bullies?	Help bullies?
Bullies need to know their behaviour is wrong, but...	... if bullies get help to solve their own problems then they won't bully any more.
Once a bully, always a bully – they'll never change, but...	... bullies need help from others to believe they can behave in a different way.
The only way to stop a bully is to make them scared of the consequences if they hurt other people, but...	... if a bully has a problem then their behaviour might be their way of trying to get attention and help from others.

Tackling teasing

If you are being picked on or teased in person and it is upsetting you, tell the people who are hurting you straight away. Sometimes people get carried away with a joke and don't realize they are being hurtful. They might be very sorry when they know how you feel. Never react by teasing or name-calling back.

Speak out

If the behaviour continues and makes you feel unhappy, the next step is to tell a teacher. Make sure they know the full story and that you explain how you feel. You could also tell a parent or another adult you trust. Talking about teasing can help, because often the nasty things people say can make you feel shy or upset. Remember to stick with the friends who make you feel good about yourself.

CASE STUDY

Omar was picked on at school for four or five years. He was called names and made to feel miserable. He reached the point where the best thing to do was to move to a different school. Now he says it was a mistake not to talk about the problem, either to the bullies or to a trusted adult. He tried to ignore the teasing but it left him feeling very unhappy. Sometimes people just don't know how much they are hurting someone else, so talking to them could solve the problem. Otherwise, he says, talk to someone you trust. You'll feel better straight away.

Don't hide your feelings
from your parents if bullying
is making you unhappy.

Getting serious

Sometimes bullying can be much more serious and talking to the bullies is not going to help. Bullying becomes a bigger problem when someone is continually abused **verbally** or **physically**, or when they are continually targeted on their mobile phone or through the internet. Some of this bullying can break the law.

If you are suffering from this type of bullying it is very important to get support. Make sure a parent or a teacher knows what is going on and follow the advice of organizations with experience in dealing with these problems. You should never suffer bullying on your own. It might feel as if the bullying is ruining your life now, but if you get help you can make it stop and learn how to move on.

There is always someone you can talk to on the end of the phone.

Online!

Many **victims** feel very alone if they are bullied at school or online and some people can start to feel as if they have no friends. Chatting to someone who has suffered similar experiences to you can make you feel much better. You might be able to help that person with their problems too. There are organizations online that let you chat to other young people who are being bullied in a safe environment. You could also email a **counsellor** who can give you helpful support and advice. You can sometimes send them text messages from your mobile phone to get some instant help. See pages 46–47 for an organization that could help you.

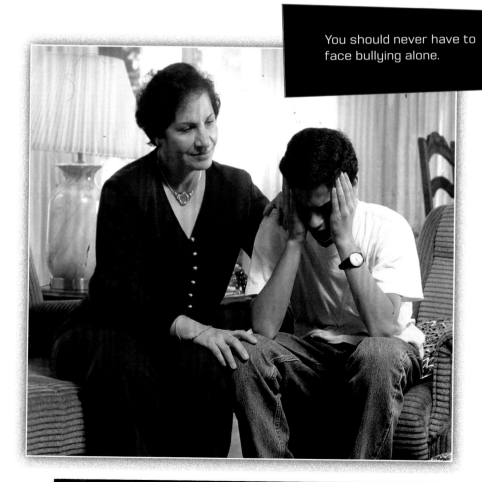

You should never have to face bullying alone.

Overcoming the bullies

All forms of bullying are harmful and upsetting. Even the smallest amount of teasing is wrong if it hurts someone. Bullies who start with name-calling and teasing can often move on to more serious bullying if they are not stopped. If a friend tells you they are being picked on, always take them seriously even if it sounds like nothing to you. If the bullying is upsetting them then treat it as a big problem. If someone tells you that your teasing is hurting them, listen to them and stop straight away.

CASE STUDY

Leila was teased about her height. She felt like she couldn't talk to anybody without them mentioning how short she was. To start with she tried to laugh it off but then she felt really upset and hurt. Her friends didn't realize how much they were hurting her by picking on her like this. Leila thinks that people should think about what they say before they speak. She wants everyone to try and accept other people for who they are, and thinks we should listen when friends ask us to stop teasing them.

Keep talking

The most important thing to remember if you are bullied is to tell a trusted adult straight away. Don't worry about upsetting your parents or feeling as though you have failed. Adults who care about you will want to help you and sharing your problem will make it feel much smaller. Together you can take a stand against the bullies.

Talking about bullying to a friend or an adult you trust will always make you feel better.

Top ten tips for coping with bullying

If you are being bullied or see bullies hurting other people, you might feel helpless. Here is a list of things to remember to help you cope and beat the bullies:

1. If you feel you are being bullied in person, confront the bully as quickly as possible. Calmly tell them to stop and let them know how they are making you feel. Then walk away.

2. If the problem carries on, record the bullying. Keep a diary of every time something happens that makes you feel bullied. You should save or print abusive text messages or emails. Be honest about what happened and who did what.

3. Tell an adult you trust about what is going on. Don't let pride or worries stop you from talking to a parent or teacher. Don't keep it to yourself because you are afraid you will upset your parents. If you speak out you might stop the bully from hurting other people and you will feel better straight away.

4. When you are using the internet, always have a trusted adult with you. If you get a nasty message, remember to "zip it, block it, and flag it" to stop **cyber** bullies in their tracks (see page 26).

5. Never leave your mobile phone lying around and only give your number to people you trust.

6. Never allow photos, videos, or sound recordings of yourself that you wouldn't want your parents to see or hear to be sent by email or text message.

7. Don't **retaliate** if you are bullied in person, on your mobile phone, or online. Never fight back or call the bully names in return because this will make things worse.

8. Remember that if you are hurt by a bully, it is the bully who is in the wrong, not you, no matter what they say to you. Talking to a trusted adult about the bullying will help you to believe this is true.

9. Talk to other young people and **counsellors** at one of the anti-bullying organizations (see pages 46– 47). They have plenty of experience and advice to help and support you. Knowing you are not alone will make you feel better.

10. Remember that most bullying stops as people grow up. You might feel that things are unbearable at the moment, but bullying does end and you will be able to put it behind you. Until then, try to spend time with family and friends who care about you and make you feel good about yourself.

Stick with the friends who make you feel happy and comfortable.

Glossary

abuse treat cruelly and cause physical or emotional harm

aggressive behaving in a forceful or threatening way that hurts other people

birthmark mark on the skin that someone has from birth

campaign series of activities or adverts to try to achieve a particular goal, such as raising people's awareness of bullying

chat room website that allows people to write messages to each other

consequence effect or result of a behaviour or action

counselling support from someone who is trained to listen and advise people who need help with problems

counsellor person who is trained to listen and advise people who need help with problems

criminal offence activity that breaks the law

cyber to do with the internet and information technology

excluded kept out of a school permanently; expelled

insecure lacking in self-confidence

intimidate frighten someone, often to force them to do something

message board website that allows people to share useful information

physical to do with the body

retaliate fight back

revenge pay someone back for something bad they have done to you

rumour gossip or story that may not be true

self-conscious when someone is very aware of how they are seen by others

social networking site online group of people who share interests and meet new friends, such as Facebook, Twitter, and MySpace

suspended kept out of school temporarily

threaten tell someone you are going to hurt or harm them

tolerate put up with something

verbal spoken

victim person who is bullied or harmed in other ways

violent acting in a way that physically hurts others

Find out more

Books

Bullies, Bigmouths and So-called Friends, Jenny Alexander
(Hodder, 2006)

Bullying (The Real Deal), Joanne Mattern (Heinemann
Library, 2008)

Bullying (Wise Guides), Michele Elliot (Hodder, 2005)

Bullying (Your Call), Deborah Chancellor (Franklin Watts, 2009)

Dont Pick On Me: How to Handle Bullying, Rosemary Stones
(Piccadilly Press, 2005)

The Seven Day Bully-Buster, Jenny Alexander (Hodder, 2007)

Websites and organizations

The following websites and organizations can offer help and
support to help you cope with bullying:

ChildLine
www.childline.org.uk
If you feel anxious or upset about being teased or bullied, you
might want to chat to someone privately. Visit the ChildLine
website or call them on 0800 1111. Calls are free and will not
appear on the phone bill. You can tell their advisors what is
worrying you and they will give you help and advice. You can
also look on the message boards to talk to other kids who are
being bullied, so you won't feel so alone.

Beatbullying

www.bbclic.com

The Beatbullying website has plenty of advice if you are being bullied. You can read about their ideas on how to lead anti-bullying campaigns, and they can even help you if you think you might be a bully.

CyberMentors

cybermentors.org.uk

Visit the CyberMentors website to talk to another young person about bullying and other problems. The website can also give you plenty of advice on staying safe online.

Bullying UK

www.bullying.co.uk

Check out the Bullying UK website, where there is a section giving support for victims of cyber bullying on the internet and through mobile phones.

Index